Collins

easy le

Spanish

Ages 7-9

¡Hola!

¿Qué tal?

Me llamo
[My name is]

Lynna Valerie Hart

How to use this book

- Look at the left-hand page first to familiarise yourself with the vocabulary being covered.

- Use the pronunciation given for each word to help you to pronounce words correctly. There are links to audio files online which will give you further support with pronunciation.

- Read out the instructions clearly and ensure children understand what they have to do.

- Discuss with the children what they have learnt.

- Recap regularly and return to previous topics that the children have enjoyed.

- Reward children with plenty of praise and encouragement.

- Encourage children to say new words out loud. This will help them to practise speaking Spanish, and help them to remember new words.

- Make learning Spanish fun for you and your children!

Special features

- Yellow boxes: introduce and outline the key vocabulary and structures in Spanish.

- Orange boxes: offer suggestions for other activities for children to consolidate their learning in different contexts.

- Orange shaded boxes: provide additional information about Spanish language and culture.

- Blue boxes: give instructions for an activity to reinforce learning.

- Audio symbols (🔊): indicate where further activities and support are available online at www.collins.co.uk/homeworkhelp

HarperCollins Publishers
Westerhill Road
Bishopbriggs
Glasgow
G64 2QT

First Edition 2019
10 9 8 7 6 5 4 3 2 1

© HarperCollins Publishers 2019

ISBN 978-0-00-831276-3

www.collins.co.uk

Printed and bound in
Great Britain by Martins the Printers

The contents of this publication are believed correct at the time of printing. Nevertheless the Publisher can accept no responsibility for errors or omissions, changes in the detail given or for any expense or loss thereby caused.

A catalogue record for this book is available from the British Library.

MANAGING EDITOR
Maree Airlie

FOR THE PUBLISHER
Laura Waddell
Sarah Woods

CONTRIBUTORS
Cristina Llompart

ILLUSTRATIONS
Q2AMedia

MAPS
© Collins Bartholomew Ltd

COVER IMAGE
Shutterstock
© Portare fortuna

Contents

Todo sobre mí
All about me

As well as being able to say hello to someone and tell them your name –
Hola, me llamo... Hello, my name is... – you may want to talk about
how old you are.

Hola, me llamo Oscar.
(Hello, my name is Oscar.)

Hola, me llamo Sofia.
(Hi, my name is Sofia.)

¿Cómo te llamas?
(What's your name?)

¿Cuántos años tienes?
(How old are you?)

Tengo ocho años. ¿Y tú?
(I'm eight. What about you?)

Tengo once años.
(I'm eleven.)

Track 1

When you are talking about your age, use the phrase **Tengo...** [**ten**goh]
which actually means **I have...** in Spanish, for example, **Tengo nueve
años**. You will be saying the equivalent of "I have nine years". It is important
to say the Spanish word **años** [**a**-nyos], otherwise you could be talking
about nine of anything! To ask someone else's age, say **¿Cuántos años
tienes?** [**kwan**tos **a**-nyos **tye**nes].

Make finger puppets or draw faces on your fingers and give each one
a name and age. Have a conversation between your fingers or with a
partner's fingers.

Did you know? In Spain, although most children start nursery school when they are 3 years old, it is
not compulsory to start until they are 6 years old. Young people can leave school when they are 16.

You are talking with your friend. Only their half of the conversation is written down. Fill in your missing greeting words and answers.

¡Hola! How are you. !

¡Cómo te llamas? Lyanna valerio Hart.

¡Cuántos años tienes? 6 years old.

¡Adiós! Good bye friend !

Draw a cartoon strip of two characters meeting and finding out about each other. You can use animals or cartoon characters if you prefer. Use the language you have been learning to write speech bubbles.

Esta es mi familia
This is my family

Part of talking about yourself is being able to say something about the people closest to you.

In Spanish, unlike in English, we do not always need to say **I** or **he** or **she** to show that we are talking about ourselves or someone else. The Spanish words themselves show who we are talking about.

So, for example, when we talk about ourselves we say **Me llamo...** and **Tengo... años**, whereas when we talk about someone else, we say **Se llama...** [seh **ya**mah] and **Tiene... años** [**tye**neh...**a**-nyos]. Can you see the difference in the Spanish words?

However, the phrase stays the same whether you are talking about a boy or a girl. So you would say **Se llama Pablo** or **Se llama Laura** and **Tiene nueve años** for both boys and girls.

When you want to introduce someone in your family, you can say **Este es mi...** [**ess**teh ess mee] (**This is my...**) if it's a boy or a man, and **Esta es mi....** [**ess**tah ess mee] (**This is my...**) if it is a girl or a woman. For example, you could say: **Este es mi padre. Se llama Diego. Tiene 37 años. (This is my dad. His name is Diego. He is 37 years old)** or **Esta es mi hermana. Se llama Clara. Tiene once años. (This is my sister. Her name is Clara. She is eleven years old).**

Make a paper people chain consisting of four or more people. Give each person a name, age and position in the family. Now describe your family of paper people to your partner.

Complete the photo ID passes below, giving the person's name and age.
Remember to use **Este es...** for men or boys, and **Esta es...** for women
and girls. You might want to complete an ID pass for one of your pets as well.

_____

Esta es mi madre.

Se llama María.

Tiene 34 años.

_____

Este es mi _____.

Se llama _____.

Tiene _____ **años.**

¿Cómo soy?
What do I look like?

If you want to describe what you look like, you can use the Spanish word **Tengo** [**ten**goh] to talk about what colour eyes you have, for example, **Tengo los ojos azules**. **I have blue eyes.** In Spanish, you put the colour word after the noun, not before it like you do in English.

Tengo los ojos...   [**ten**goh los ohos]   **I have ... eyes.**

azules [ah**thu**les] **blue**   **verdes** [**bair**des] **green**   **castaños** [kas**tah**nyos] **hazel**   **negros** [**neh**gros] **black**

Although the word for brown in Spanish is usually **marrón**, Spanish uses another word to describe brown hair and brown eyes: **castaño** [kas**ta**hnyio].

To describe the colour and style of your hair, use the same phrase **Tengo** with some of the words given below. You put the Spanish colour word after the noun as before, for example, **Tengo el pelo largo y castaño** **I have long brown hair.**

Tengo el pelo...   [**ten**goh el **peh**lo]   **I have...hair.**

castaño [kas**tah**nyo] **brown**   **negro** [**neh**groh] **black**   **rubio** [**ruh**byo] **blonde**

corto [**kor**toh] **short**   **largo** [**lar**goh] **long**   **rizado** [ree**thah**doh] **curly**   **liso** [**lee**soh] **straight**

Play "**¿Quién es así?**" with a partner. Think of someone you both know well and describe yourself as that person using **Tengo...**, for example: **Tengo el pelo rubio y corto. Tengo los ojos castaños**. Your partner has to guess who you are describing. You could also describe characters from certain films, or even celebrities.

Draw a picture of your best friend in the box below. Answer the questions given below to write about him or her in Spanish. Remember that you use **este es** to say **this is** for boys and **esta es** to say **this is** for girls, so you can cross out the word you don't need.

¿Quién es esta?/
¿Quién es este?
Who is this?

Esta es/Este es_____

¿Cómo es?
What does she/he look like?

Tiene los ojos _____

Tiene el pelo_____

Cómo me siento
How I feel

When someone asks **¿Qué tal?** [**keh** tal] or **¿Cómo estás?** [**koh**moh ess**tass**], it is useful to know a few phrases to describe how you are feeling.

Estoy enfadado.

[ess**toy** enfah**dah**doh]

I'm angry.

Estoy triste.

[ess**toy** **trees**teh]

I'm sad.

Estoy contenta.

[ess**toy** kon**ten**tah]

I'm happy.

Estoy cansada.

[ess**toy** kan**sah**dah]

I'm tired.

Tengo hambre.

[**te**ngoh **am**breh]

I'm hungry.

Tengo sed.

[**ten**goh seth]

I'm thirsty.

In general, if you want to say how you are feeling, you can use **Estoy...** [ess**toy**] **I am...** with an adjective, for example, **enfermo** [en**feh**rmo] meaning **ill**, **aburrido** [ahbu**rree**doh] meaning **bored**, and so on. Some adjectives end in **a** if you are a girl and in **o** if you are a boy. For example, if you are a girl you will say that you are **contenta** or **cansada**, but if you are a boy you will say **contento** or **cansado**.

 Track 2

Use paper plates to draw faces showing different emotions. Your partner asks **¿Qué tal?** and you show one of your "faces" and say how you are feeling.

Write underneath each image how that person is feeling using **Estoy...** or **Tengo...** If you use **Estoy**, remember to use the adjective ending **a** for a girl or **o** for a boy.

_____

_____

_____

_____

_____

_____

El tiempo
The weather

We all like to talk about the weather and these phrases will help you to answer the question: **¿Qué tiempo hace?** [**ke tyem**poh **ah**theh] **What's the weather like?**

Llueve.
[**yue**veh]
It's raining.

Hace sol.
[**ah**the sol]
It's sunny.

Hace viento.
[**ah**the **byen**toh]
It's windy.

Está nublado.
[ess**ta** noo**blah**doh]
It's cloudy.

Hace calor.
[**ah**the kah**lor**]
It's hot.

Hace frío.
[**ah**the **free**oh]
It's cold.

Look out of the window – how would you describe the weather today? **Hoy...** [oy] **Today it...** Now look up some countries in other parts of the world on the internet and describe the weather there.

Did you know? In the very north of Spain, the weather can be very similar to the UK. However, in central and southern Spain it can be very hot in the summer, sometimes over 40 °C.

Use the outline map of Spain below to draw your own weather map using traditional weather symbols. Complete the sentences below the map with the appropriate weather phrases. Practise saying the weather report to a partner; maybe you could even record or film yourself saying it?

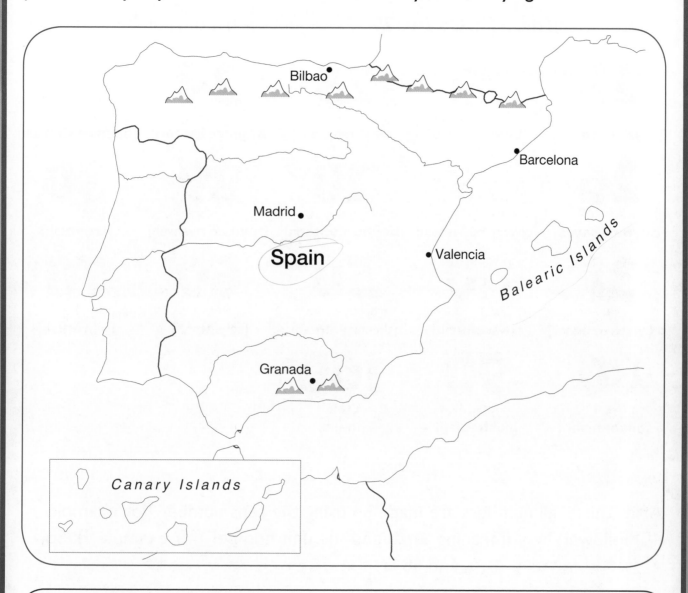

En Madrid _____

En Granada _____

En Barcelona _____

En Bilbao _____

En Valencia _____

Los números hasta 100
Numbers to 100

After learning the numbers 1 to 20, it's useful to learn the numbers after 20.

21 veintiuno [**beyn**tee **oo**noh]

22 veintidós [**beyn**tee doss]

23 veintitrés [**beyn**tee trehs]

24 veinticuatro [**beyn**tee **kwa**tro]

25 veinticinco [**beyn**tee **thin**koh]

26 veintiséis [**beyn**tee **sayss**]

27 veintisiete [**beyn**tee see-**eh**teh]

28 veintiocho [**beyn**tee **oh**choh]

29 veintinueve [**beyn**tee **nwe**veh]

30 treinta [**treyn**tah]

31 treinta y uno [**treyn**tah ee **oo**noh]

40 cuarenta [kwa**rehn**tah]

50 cincuenta [theen**kwen**tah]

60 sesenta [seh**sen**tah]

70 setenta [seh**ten**tah]

80 ochenta [oh**chen**tah]

90 noventa [noh**ben**tah]

100 cien [thyen]

After thirty, all numbers are made up using the tens number (for example 40) followed by **y** (meaning **and**) and the unit number (for example 1). So, 41 is **cuarenta y uno**, and 68 is **sesenta y ocho**.

Practise counting in tens, backwards and forwards, loudly and quietly, slowly and quickly. You could try saying your ten times table in Spanish, for example, **cinco por diez es igual a, cincuenta**.

Did you know? In Spain people often say their telephone numbers in pairs or groups of three numbers, rather than singly like we do, for example: the phone number 913456789 would be said in Spanish as: 91-345-67-89 (ninety-one, three hundred and forty-five, sixty-seven, eighty-nine). Like in the UK, the first two or three digits of a landline number are called the prefix and show where the person lives. For example, the prefix for Madrid is 91, and the prefix for Cádiz is 956.

Work out the sums and write the answers in Spanish. Then colour in **el robot** using the colour key provided.

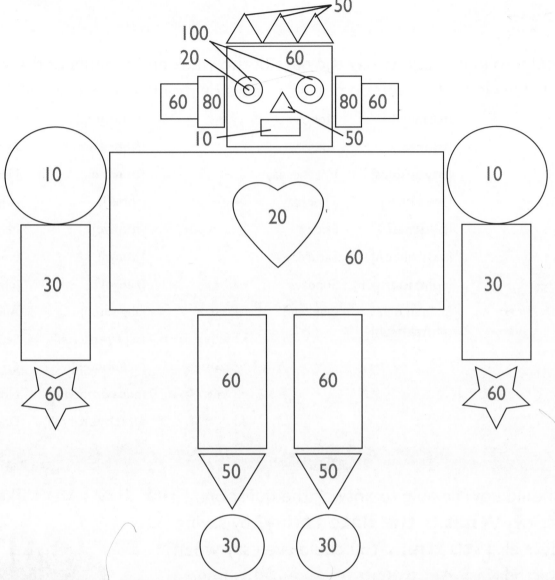

El cálculo	...es igual a...	...el color...
(más = add; menos = take away)	(equals)	
diez *más* veinte		verde
sesenta *menos* cuarenta		rojo
treinta *menos* veinte		naranja
cuarenta *más* cuarenta		violeta
setenta *más* treinta		negro
setenta *menos* veinte		amarillo
cincuenta *más* diez		azul

Los días de la semana/Los meses
Days of the week/Months

It is useful to know how to say the days of the week and months of the year in Spanish. Unlike English, you do not write days or months with a capital letter.

lunes	[**luh**ness]	Monday	enero	[eh**neh**roh]	January
martes	[**mar**tes]	Tuesday	febrero	[feh**breh**roh]	February
miércoles	[**myer**koles]	Wednesday	marzo	[**mar**thoh]	March
jueves	[**hweh**bes]	Thursday	abril	[ah**bril**]	April
viernes	[**byer**nes]	Friday	mayo	[**mah**yo]	May
sábado	[**sah**bahdoh]	Saturday	junio	[**hu**nyo]	June
domingo	[doh**meen**goh]	Sunday	julio	[**hu**lyo]	July
el fin de semana	[el feen deh seh**mah**nah]	weekend	agosto	[ah**gos**toh]	August
			septiembre	[sep**tyem**breh]	September
			octubre	[oc**tuh**breh]	October
			noviembre	[no**byem**breh]	November
			diciembre	[dee**thyem**breh]	December

You should now be able to answer the question: **¿Qué día es hoy?** [keh dya ess oy] **What is the date today?** by saying **Es el...** [ess el...] **It's the...** You could even say when your birthday is: **Mi cumpleaños es el...** [mee kumpleh-**an**yios ess el] **My birthday is the...**

 Track 4

Write out the names of days of the week and months on separate pieces of paper. Mix them up and then try to put them back into the correct order as quickly as possible. You could also challenge your partner to beat your time.

Did you know? As well as their birthdays, Spanish people sometimes celebrate their "name day" called **el santo** which means the saint day.

Juego: Sopa de letras

Can you find some of the days of the week and the months in Spanish in the square opposite?

lunes ✓   marzo ✓

octubre ✓   viernes ✓

enero ✓   mayo ✓

martes ✓   domingo ✓

julio ✓   jueves ✓

O	Q	G	H	Q	R	U	X	L	Y
C	J	M	A	R	T	E	S	L	X
T	U	A	M	Y	W	O	A	U	A
U	E	N	E	R	O	Z	D	N	D
B	V	D	V	I	E	R	N	E	S
R	E	D	H	A	J	A	I	S	O
E	S	O	N	I	Q	M	D	A	Y
P	D	O	M	I	N	G	O	P	A
K	J	N	C	P	L	U	A	A	M
J	U	L	I	O	E	T	J	H	S

Why not make up your own **Sopa de letras** using some of the Spanish words for months or days of the week?

_____

_____

_____

_____

_____

¿Qué te gusta hacer?
What do you like doing?

If you want to talk about what you like in Spanish you can use the phrase **Me gusta** [meh **goos**ta] **I like...**, for example, **Me gusta el fin de semana**. You can also say what you don't like by learning the phrase: **No me gusta...** [noh meh **goos**ta] **I don't like...**, for example, **No me gusta enero.** If you feel even more strongly, you can say **Me encanta** [me en**kan**tah] **I love...** and **Odio...** [**oh**dyo] **I hate...**

When talking to someone in Spanish you might want to say what kinds of things you enjoy doing or don't enjoy doing.

Me gusta.../No me gusta...

nadar
[nah**dar**]
swimming

montar en bicicleta
[mon**tar** en bithee**kle**tah]
cycling

jugar al fútbol
[hu**gar** al **foot**bol]
playing football

leer
[leh-**er**]
reading

dibujar
[deebuh**har**]
drawing

jugar a los videojuegos
[hu**gar** a los beedeho**hweh**gos]
playing video games

Work with a partner: one person says what they like or don't like doing using **Me gusta...** or **No me gusta...** The other person has to mime the activity described, but only if their partner likes doing it. If they don't like doing it, you don't mime it, so listen carefully!

CONTENTS

ABOUT THIS BOOK

This workbook is written primarily for use in a group situation, but can easily be used by individuals who want to study the biblical picture of God. It can be used in a variety of contexts, so it is perhaps helpful to spell out the assumptions that we have made about the groups that will use it. These can have a variety of names – home groups, Bible study groups, cell groups – we've used housegroup as the generic term.

▶ The emphasis of the studies will be on the application of the Bible. Group members will not just learn facts, but will be encouraged to think: 'How does this apply to me? What change does it require of me? What incidents or situations in my life is this relevant to?'

▶ Housegroups can encourage honesty and make space for questions and doubts. The aim of the studies is not to find the 'right answer' but to help members understand the Bible by working through the questions. The Christian faith throws up paradoxes. Events in people's lives may make particular verses difficult to understand. The housegroup should be a safe place to express these concerns.

▶ Housegroups can give opportunities for deep friendships to develop. Group members will be encouraged to talk about their experiences, feelings, questions, hopes and fears. They will be able to offer one another pastoral support and to get involved in each other's lives.

▶ There is a difference between being a collection of individuals who happen to meet together every Wednesday and being an effective group who bounce ideas off each other, spark inspiration and creativity and pool their talents and resources to create solutions together and whose whole is definitely greater than the sum of its parts. The process of working through these studies will encourage healthy group dynamics.

Space is given for you to write answers, comments, questions and thoughts. This book will not tell you what to think, but will help you to discover the truth of God's word through thinking, discussing, praying and listening.

FOR GROUP MEMBERS

▶ You will get more out of the study if you spend some time during the week reading the passage and thinking about the questions. Make a note of anything you don't understand.

▶ Pray that God will help you to understand the passage and show you how to apply it. Pray for other members in the group too, that they will find the study helpful.

● Be willing to take part in the discussions. The leader of the group is not there as an expert with all the answers. They will want everyone to get involved and share their thoughts and opinions.

▶ However, don't dominate the group! If you are aware that you are saying a lot, make space for others to contribute. Be sensitive to other group members and aim to be encouraging. If you disagree with someone, say so but without putting down their contribution.

FOR INDIVIDUALS

▶ Although this book is written with a group in mind, it can also be easily used by individuals. You obviously won't be able to do the group activities suggested, but you can consider how you would answer the questions and write your thoughts in the space provided.

● You may find it helpful to talk to a prayer partner about what you have learnt, and ask them to pray for you as you try and apply what you are learning to your life.

▶ The New International Version of the text is printed in the book. If you usually use a different version, then read from your own Bible as well.

INTRODUCTION

YAHWEH – GOD IN ALL HIS FULLNESS

So what is the God you believe in really like? Is he distant and vague, like a complicated scientific formula, or a kind of benevolent Father Christmas? Do you run to him in trouble, as a toddler runs to Daddy, or practically ignore him like a teenager in a mood? Is he controlling the universe as a chess master controls the board, or is he letting it go to rack and ruin, just an abandoned project? Is God an integral part of your sleep/work/eat/sleep day-to-day lifestyle or does he just pop up on Sunday mornings?

The Bible paints an awesome picture of God. In fact, it is so amazing we would need all eternity to know God in all his fullness: his perfection, power and love are infinite and his glory is incomprehensible. And yet the Bible also teaches us that we are to be like God: that is, godly. What an incredible challenge, especially in our comfortable, secular world.

In order to get to know God more and to become more like him, we need to commit ourselves to learning about the God of the Bible – God in all his fullness. Here is what the great preacher C.H. Spurgeon said about this task:

> The highest science, the loftiest speculation, the mightiest philosophy, which can ever engage the attention of a child of God, is the name, the nature, the person, the work, the doings and the existence of the great God whom he calls his father.[1]

Following Spurgeon's cue, this book seeks to guide you into a deeper grasp of the magnificence of God. In the following studies, you will explore seven snapshots from Scripture that highlight different aspects of God's nature.

These glimpses of God will show that even mighty heroes of the faith needed a renewed vision of God. Moses needed a revelation of God in order to lead God's people through the dangers of the desert to the Promised Land; David needed to remember God's generosity to ignite his praise for God; the apostle John needed a vision of God to sustain him in prison on Patmos and the early church held onto God's faithfulness as they prepared to stand firm against persecution. If they needed a sharper focus on God, how much more do we need to set ourselves to the task of gaining a bigger picture of God through the Scriptures to sustain us in our daily lives and to teach us worship and godliness. We pray that as you study God's word and catch glimpses of Yahweh in all his fullness, you may grow in your love and worship for God and reflect his glory to the world.

[1] Spurgeon, *The New Park Street Pulpit*, vol. 1, (Banner of Truth, 1963) p1

THE CREATOR GOD

Aim: To discover God as our Creator and our place in his creation

TO SET THE SCENE

In teams, set a challenge to build the tallest tower out of LEGO® bricks, newspaper or tins. Afterwards discuss how you felt about your design, resources and finished products.

READ THE PASSAGE TOGETHER

In the beginning God created the heavens and the earth. Now the earth was formless and empty, darkness was over the surface of the deep, and the Spirit of God was hovering over the waters.

And God said,'Let there be light', and there was light. God saw that the light was good, and he separated the light from the darkness. God called the light 'day' and the darkness he called 'night'. And there was evening and there was morning—the first day.

And God said 'Let there be a vault between the waters to separate water from water.' So God made the vault and separated the water under the vault from the water above it. And it was so. God called the vault 'sky' and there was evening and there was morning—the second day.

And God said, 'Let the water under the sky be gathered to one place, and let dry ground appear.' And it was so. God called the dry ground 'land', and the gathered waters he called 'seas'. And God saw that it was good.

Then God said, 'Let the land produce vegetation: seed-bearing plants and trees on the land that bear fruit with seed in it, according to their various kinds.' And it was so. The land produced vegetation; plants bearing seeds according to their kinds and trees bearing fruit with seed in it according to their kinds. And God saw that it was good. And there was evening, and there was morning—the third day.

And God said, 'Let there be lights in the vault of the sky to separate the day from the night, and let them serve as signs to mark seasons and days and years, and let them be lights in the vault of the sky to give light on the earth.' And it was so. God made two great lights—the greater light to govern the day and the lesser light to govern the night. He also made the stars. God set them in the vault of the sky to give light on the earth, to govern the day and the night, and to separate light from darkness. And God saw that it was good. And there was evening, and there was morning—the fourth day.

And God said, 'Let the water teem with living creatures, and let birds fly above the earth, across the vault of the sky.' So God created the great creatures of the sea and every living and moving thing with which the water teems, according to their kinds, and every winged bird according to its kind. And God saw that it was good. God blessed them and said, 'Be fruitful and increase in number and fill the water in the seas, and let the birds increase on the earth.' And there was evening, and there was morning—the fifth day.

And God said, 'Let the land produce living creatures according to their kind; livestock, creatures that move along the ground, and wild animals, each according to its kind.' And it was so. God made the wild animals according to their kinds, the livestock according to their kinds, and all the creatures that move along the ground according to their kinds, and God saw that it was good.

And God said, 'Let us make human beings in our own image, in our likeness, so that they may rule over the fish in the sea and the birds in the sky, over the livestock and all the wild animals, and over all the creatures that move along the ground.'

So God created human beings in his own image, in the image of God he created them; male and female he created them. God blessed them and said to them, 'Be fruitful and increase in number; fill the earth and subdue it. Rule over the fish in the sea and the birds in the sky and over every living creature that moves along the ground.' Then God said, 'I give you every seed-bearing plant on the face of the whole earth and every tree that has fruit with seed in it. They will be yours for food. And to all the beasts of the earth and the birds in the sky and all the creatures that move on the ground—everything that has breath of life in it—I give every green plant for food.' And it was so God saw all that he had made, and it was very good. And there was evening, and there was morning—the sixth day.

Genesis 1:1–31

1. God is described as creating the entire universe simply by speaking. In verse 16 we are told 'He also made the stars.' How do you feel as you reflect on God's creative power?

2. Look at what God does on the first three days of creation and on the second three days of creation. What parallels can you find?

3. What are the significant differences between the description of the creation of human beings and the rest of creation?

4. What does it mean that humanity is made in the image of God (v26)? Which of the following is closest to the truth?

    a) We physically resemble God
    b) Our personality mirrors God's
    c) We are gods
    d) We represent God

ENGAGING WITH THE WORLD **5.** Who is made in the image of God? How should this affect the way we treat people from differing cultures, economic backgrounds, sexualities and abilities?

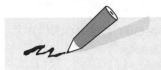

ENGAGING WITH THE WORLD **6.** Some would read verses 27–28 as a mandate for us to exploit planet Earth, others believe that we are to care for the planet above human life.
What do you think?

ENGAGING WITH THE WORLD **7.** There is a man standing on a ledge fifteen floors up. Below him a crowd has gathered. The man cries out 'What is the point of life?' How would you reply?

SCIENCE VERSUS RELIGION?

Many Christians feel nervous about the opening chapters of Genesis because they have been told that science has disproved the Bible. In fact, Christianity has provided the intellectual framework in which science has flourished. Atheistic scientists have no reason to expect the universe to be rational or intelligible but pursue scientific investigations in faith, expecting there to be answers. Christians have always believed that God created the universe and therefore we could learn about him through investigating the Scriptures and the creation.

Another reason for Christians to feel nervous when approaching Genesis 1 is that even the Christian community is divided over whether the Genesis account is a literal description of God's creation of the world in six 24-hour periods or whether it is a literary device. Some evangelicals believe that God used evolution for his ends, while others dismiss this as worldly compromise. There remains a great deal of debate in these circles. However, all Christians are united in the belief that God is the ultimate Creator of the universe.

---

8. Divide the group into two and ask one side to build a case for six day creation and the other to argue for a literary interpretation of Genesis 1.

9. Your neighbour believes that the universe exists by pure chance and evolution. What questions would you ask them to try to open their mind to another view?

HOW DOES THIS **APPLY TO ME** **10.** When you look in the mirror, how does knowing that God created you change the way you view yourself?

WORSHIP

Read Psalm 19.

Our friend Beth is inspired to worship God when she sees a newborn baby's feet. My mother-in-law is inspired by the Welsh mountains. Which part of creation most inspires you to worship God?

Read, sing or listen to a CD version of *O Lord my God, when I in awesome wonder* or another song that speaks of worshipping God the Creator.

DURING THE WEEK

Ask as many friends and neighbours as possible about their beliefs regarding the origins of the universe. Use this as an opportunity to listen to others, to build relationships and, if appropriate, to share the gospel.

Watch the news. Reflect on how many of the problems in the world would be alleviated if we lived out the fact that the world belongs to God and that all human beings are made in his image. What three things would make your lifestyle reflect this more?

FOR FURTHER STUDY

Read Romans 1:18–23. Think about how you see God's invisible qualities, eternal power and divine nature through the world God has made.

Books to read[1]

Ruth Valerio	*L is for lifestyle*	IVP
David Wilkinson	*God, the Big Bang and Stephen Hawking*	Monarch
Henri Blocher	*In the beginning*	IVP

1 Books are listed in order of complexity – the most accessible first!

THE HOLY GOD

AIM

Aim: To learn to depend on a holy God and experience his presence in every situation

TO SET THE SCENE

Show a clip or trailer from the film *Lost in Translation* or *Castaway* (or an alternative clip showing loneliness). Ask the group to parallel these experiences of 'lostness' with times when they have felt most alone.

READ THE PASSAGE TOGETHER

Moses said to the LORD, "You have been telling me, 'Lead these people,' but you have not let me know whom you will send with me. You have said, 'I know you by name and you have found favour with me.' If you are pleased with me, teach me your ways so I may know you and continue to find favour with you. Remember that this nation is your people."

The LORD replied, "My Presence will go with you, and I will give you rest."

Then Moses said to him, "If your Presence does not go with us, do not send us up from here. How will anyone know that you are pleased with me and with your people unless you go with us? What else will distinguish me and your people from all the other people on the face of the earth?"

And the LORD said to Moses, "I will do the very thing you have asked, because I am pleased with you and I know you by name."

Then Moses said, "Now show me your glory."

And the LORD said, "I will cause all my goodness to pass in front of you, and I will proclaim my name, the LORD, in your presence. I will have mercy on whom I will have mercy, and I will have compassion on whom I will have compassion. But," he said, "you cannot see my face, for no-one may see me and live."

Then the LORD said, "There is a place near me where you may stand on a rock. When my glory passes by, I will put you in a cleft in the rock and cover you with my hand until I have passed by. Then I will remove my hand and you will see my back; but my face must not be seen."

*So Moses chiselled out two stone tablets like the first ones and went up Mount Sinai early in the morning, as the L*ORD* had commanded him; and he carried the two stone tablets in his hands. Then the L*ORD* came down in the cloud and stood there with him and proclaimed his name, the L*ORD*. And he passed in front of Moses, proclaiming, "The L*ORD*, the L*ORD*, the compassionate and gracious God, slow to anger, abounding in love and faithfulness, maintaining love to thousands, and forgiving wickedness, rebellion and sin. Yet he does not leave the guilty unpunished; he punishes the children and their children for the sin of the fathers to the third and fourth generation."*

Moses bowed to the ground at once and worshipped. "O Lord, if I have found favour in your eyes," he said, "then let the Lord go with us. Although this is a stiff-necked people, forgive our wickedness and our sin, and take us as your inheritance."

*Then the L*ORD* said: "I am making a covenant with you. Before all your people I will do wonders never before done in any nation in all the world. The people you live among will see how awesome is the work that I, the L*ORD*, will do for you. Obey what I command you today. I will drive out before you the Amorites, Canaanites, Hittites, Perizzites, Hivites and Jebusites. Be careful not to make a treaty with those who live in the land where you are going, or they will be a snare among you. Break down their altars, smash their sacred stones and cut down their Asherah poles. Do not worship any other god, for the L*ORD*, whose name is Jealous, is a jealous God.*

Exodus 33:12 – 34:14

ABOUT THE BOOK OF EXODUS

Exodus describes Israel's exit from Egypt. Despite God's blessing of Egypt through his servant Joseph, Exodus begins with the nation of Israel in slavery, facing ethnic cleansing, as the order is given to execute a whole generation of male babies. God rescues Moses and calls him to lead his people out of Egypt and into the Promised Land. Although Israel left Egypt overnight, the process of getting Egypt out of Israel took forty years. This incredible transformation of a nation in preparation for the Promised Land is recorded in great detail in Exodus. God demonstrates his incredible patience with a nation that seems to do nothing but grumble, doubt his sovereignty and even worship a false god.

God's holiness is particularly emphasised in this book. When Moses is called by God at the burning bush, he is commanded to remove his sandals as he is on holy ground. The law of God is given from God's holy mountain and calls people to be holy as God is Holy. The intricate design of the tabernacle also centres on the presence of God in the 'Most Holy Place.'

1. Leadership is often described as the loneliest job. Scanning over the previous chapters of Exodus, discuss why Moses might have found leading the nation of Israel particularly lonely.

2. In his loneliness, Moses craves the presence of God (33:14–15). What reasons does Moses give for asking to see God's glory? Where do you go when you feel lonely? How does Moses' example challenge us?

3. How do we use the word 'glory' today? How does God describe his glory in 33:19–20? Why does Moses need to be protected from God's glory?

HOW DOES THIS **4.** In C.S. Lewis's classic *The Lion, the Witch and the Wardrobe*, Lucy famously asks if Aslan is tame and is told 'He is not tame but **APPLY TO ME** he is good.' Some Christians are over-familiar with God. Others relate to God only with a sense of fear and terror. Which trap are you most likely to fall into? What can we do to fear God and yet enjoy intimacy with him?

5. How does God describe himself in 34:5−7? Which of these characteristics do you find most comforting and which most challenging?

6. How does Moses react to this vision of God's glory? What is the significance of what he asks for? What is God's promise to Moses?

7. How would you respond to someone who said: 'God is behaving like a power-hungry dictator when he asks for obedience and like a jealous boyfriend when he asks for exclusive loyalty'?

HOW DOES THIS

APPLY TO ME

8. One day we will all see God face to face (1 Cor. 13:12). After studying Moses' encounter with God, how do you feel about this prospect?

GRACE OR LEGALISM?

Over the ages the church has often swung between emphasising God's grace and his holiness. Sometimes emphasising God's grace has led to a disregard for personal holiness; conversely focussing on God's holiness has often led to legalism.

In the difficult middle path we need to recognise that God deserves nothing less than our total allegiance and wholehearted obedience. However, we need to be firmly rooted in the truth that our relationship with God is solely based on God's free gift of grace, not on our achievements.

ENGAGING WITH

THE WORLD

9. In recognition of God's grace to you, think of something gracious you could do for a friend this week. For example: bake a cake for your next door neighbour, offer to babysit for a family at church, send a postcard to somebody you have lost touch with or give them a ring.

ENGAGING WITH

THE WORLD

10. Based on today's study, what would you say to the following people:

'I am too bad to become a Christian. I could never measure up to God's standards.'

'I don't need to become a Christian. I live a good life and help others whenever I can.'

WORSHIP
Read Psalm 139:1-12.

Moses was empowered to fulfil the lonely task of leading God's people because he knew God's presence was with him wherever he went. List all the places you need to go tomorrow and think of practical and creative things you could do today to help you remind yourself of God's presence. For example: put a post-it note on the bathroom mirror with a verse from Psalm 139 or put a Bible in your briefcase to leave at work or buy the *Big Issue* from the homeless person you normally pass while shopping. You could even buy them a hot drink.

We will only truly see God's glory in heaven. But in this life we are given glimpses of his majesty. Worship God for the glimpses of glory you have experienced in the last week.

DURING THE WEEK
In Exodus 34:6-7 there are seven characteristics of God that are mentioned. Take one of these a day, memorise it, meditate on it and consider how we can reflect this aspect of God's character.

Day 1	Compassionate	Day 2	Gracious
Day 3	Slow to anger	Day 4	Abounding in love
Day 5	Abounding in faithfulness	Day 6	Maintaining love to thousands
Day 7	Forgiving wickedness, rebellion and sin		

We have noted how lonely the job of leadership can be. Think of practical ways you might be able to encourage the leaders in your church, in your place of work and in your community.

FOR FURTHER STUDY
Read the accounts of people who see God's glory in Scripture. What similarities do you notice?

Exodus 3	Moses
Isaiah 6:1-13	Isaiah
Revelation 1:12-20	John

Books to read:

J. Bridges	*The pursuit of holiness*	Navpress
A.W. Tozer	*The knowledge of the Holy*	STL
J.I. Packer	*A passion for holiness*	Crossway
B. Trevethan	*The beauty of God's holiness*	IVP

THE TRUE GOD

Aim: To recognise that God alone is worthy of our total allegiance

TO SET THE SCENE

If you were to make a time capsule to be opened in 25 years' time in your church, what would you put in it?

READ THE PASSAGE TOGETHER

These are the commands, decrees and laws the LORD your God directed me to teach you to observe in the land that you are crossing the Jordan to possess, so that you, your children and their children after them may fear the LORD your God as long as you live by keeping all his decrees and commands that I give you, and so that you may enjoy long life. Hear, O Israel, and be careful to obey so that it may go well with you and that you may increase greatly in a land flowing with milk and honey, just as the LORD, the God of your fathers, promised you.

Hear, O Israel: The LORD our God, the LORD is one. Love the LORD your God with all your heart and with all your soul and with all your strength. These commandments that I give you today are to be upon your hearts. Impress them on your children. Talk about them when you sit at home and when you walk along the road, when you lie down and when you get up. Tie them as symbols on your hands and bind them on your foreheads. Write them on the doorframes of your houses and on your gates.

When the LORD your God brings you into the land he swore to your fathers, to Abraham, Isaac and Jacob, to give you—a land with large, flourishing cities you did not build, houses filled with all kinds of good things you did not provide, wells you did not dig, and vineyards and olive groves you did not plant—then when you eat and are satisfied, be careful that you do not forget the LORD, who brought you out of Egypt, out of the land of slavery.

Fear the LORD your God, serve him only and take your oaths in his name. Do not follow other gods, the gods of the peoples around you; for the LORD your God, who is among you, is a jealous God and his anger will burn against you, and he will destroy you from the face of the land. Do not test the LORD your God as you did at Massah. Be sure to keep the commands of the LORD your God and the stipulations and decrees he has given you. Do what is right and good in the LORD's sight, so that it may go well with you and you may go in and take over the good land that the LORD promised on oath to your forefathers, thrusting out all your enemies before you, as the LORD said.

In the future, when your son asks you, "What is the meaning of the stipulations, decrees and laws the LORD our God has commanded you?" tell him: "We were slaves of Pharaoh in Egypt, but the LORD brought us out of Egypt with a mighty hand. Before our eyes the LORD sent miraculous signs and wonders—great and terrible—upon Egypt and Pharaoh and his whole household. But he brought us out from there to bring us in and give us the land that he promised on oath to our forefathers. The LORD commanded us to obey all these decrees and to fear the LORD our God, so that we might always prosper and be kept alive, as is the case today. And if we are careful to obey all this law before the LORD our God, as he has commanded us, that will be our righteousness."

Deuteronomy 6:1–25

ABOUT THE BOOK OF DEUTERONOMY
This is the last will and testament of Moses. Standing on the brink of entering the Promised Land, Moses spells out the implications of the law one more time (Deuteronomy means literally 'second law'), knowing that he will not be making those final steps with the people he has led out of Egypt and through the wilderness. Moses realises that the people will struggle with the transition from being a nation on the move to being established in a land, and that they may be tempted to forget God. The encouragement to remember God is a key theme in this book. Moses also knows that they will come across people groups who worship other gods, and so he pleads with them to remain faithful to the one true God.

Deuteronomy has a pivotal place in the Bible. The Old Testament prophets continually call people back to obey the laws in this book and Jesus himself, when facing his epic spiritual battle with the devil in the desert, quotes from this book to ward off and ultimately defeat his tempter.

Similarly to the Israelites, we too are becoming settled in an affluent and multicultural society and so we need to hear Moses' challenge to us to not put our confidence in our circumstances but to continue to trust the one true God.

 APPLY THIS TO **1.** What are the main challenges facing Christians today that are unique to this generation? What new challenges will the next **MY CHURCH** generation face?

2. God has brought the nation of Israel out of slavery through the wilderness and finally into a land that is materially blessed. Should we claim this as God's will for us as individuals, or as a nation, or not at all?

3. Moses highlights two dangers for the settlers in the Promised Land (vv10–19). What are they and in what ways are they relevant for us today?

4. Moses is eager to equip the people to face these challenges. What strategy does he use in verses 1–9? What does he emphasise and what practical suggestions does he make?

5. Verse 4 is known as the Shema (the Hebrew word for 'Hear') and still forms part of the Jewish daily prayer routine. Discuss why it says 'The Lord is one.' Does it mean:

- ▶ The Trinity does not yet exist?
- ▶ There is only one God?
- ▶ Everyone worships the same God?
- ▶ The God of the Promised Land is the same God who led them from Israel?
- ▶ God is the only object of worship?

 ENGAGING WITH **6.** Play a game. Divide into two teams. Which team can make the longest list of popular songs containing the word 'Love' in **THE WORLD** the title? What do these songs tell us about our culture's understanding of the word 'love'? How does this compare with the command to love God in verse 5?

7. How would you answer the following people:

a) 'If I were to love God with all my heart, soul and strength, there would be no love left for anything else'

b) 'I used to love God with all my heart, soul and strength, but as I have matured, I am less fanatical, which I think is good.'

8. In verse 6 Moses is referring to the Ten Commandments as well as the previous verse. List the different ways these commandments are to be integrated into our lives (vv6–9). Which of these are directly relevant for us today? Which do we need to rediscover in our culture?

LOOK CLOSELY AT WHERE GOD'S LAW SHOULD BE

On our hearts – Reading God's word must not simply be an intellectual or social affair but should affect our emotional life and deepest being.

On your children – Passing on the faith is a family responsibility.

On your lips – Bible study should not just be an individual pastime. We need to discuss it with others.

On your hands – Many Jewish people take this literally and tie boxes (phylacteries) to their hands, foreheads and door-frames. Alternatively we can understand this metaphorically, by practising God's laws in whatever we are doing.

On your foreheads – we should be studying and meditating on God's word continually.

On your door-posts – we need to be reminded of God's laws when we enter the house and embark on family life and when we leave the house and engage with the world.

HOW DOES THIS APPLY TO ME **9.** Thinking back to your own childhood, who influenced you most spiritually? What could you do practically to pass the faith on to the next generation, in your church or your family?

ENGAGING WITH THE WORLD **10.** Whilst in conversation, somebody comments 'All this fuss about different religions – there is only one God.' How does this make you feel? What would be a tactful and helpful way to reply?

WORSHIP

What stops us from giving God the wholehearted devotion he requires from us? Pray for each other in pairs, and offer to call your partner during the week to find out how they are doing.

This passage teaches us not that worship is to be part of our lives but that life is to be part of our worship. This frees us to understand that we can show our love for God while we are driving to work, cooking the dinner or helping a friend.

Memorise Colossians 3:23.

Read, sing or listen to devotional songs such as *You are worthy of all my praise* (Jeremy Camp), *There is none like you* (Michael W. Smith) or *Heart of worship* (Matt Redman)

DURING THE WEEK

Spend some time reviewing your credit card statement or bank statement from last month. What do your spending habits tell you about your priorities?

Look over your diary for the month ahead. If a non-Christian friend were to see it, who or what would they think is important to you?

Keep a record of how you spend each hour over a day. How does God fit into your schedule? Do you need to make any changes?

The Jewish habit of physically carrying around important parts of Scripture can be useful to us too. Think of three different places where you could put some verses of Scripture; for example, as the screensaver for your computer, as an insert for your wallet or a key fob.

FOR FURTHER STUDY

Read Luke 4:1-13. How does Jesus use Deuteronomy to protect himself from the devil's lies?

Read Romans 12 and compare it with today's passage.

Books to read:

Michael Green	*Don't all roads lead to God?*	IVP
Ravi Zacharias	*Jesus amongst other gods:*	
	the absolute truth of the Christian message	STL

THE FAITHFUL GOD

Aim: To transform our worship from apathy to passion by recognising God's faithfulness in our lives

TO SET THE SCENE

Play a memory game with twenty small random items on a tray. Allow the group to see the tray for thirty seconds and then cover it. Ask the group to write down individually what they remember. Provide a prize as an incentive. Use this as a discussion starter about how people rate their memories and the things that they find it easiest to remember.

READ THE PASSAGE TOGETHER

Praise the LORD, O my soul;
all my inmost being, praise his holy name.
Praise the LORD, O my soul,
and forget not all his benefits–
who forgives all your sins
and heals all your diseases,
who redeems your life from the pit
and crowns you with love and compassion,
who satisfies your desires with good things
so that your youth is renewed like the eagle's.
The LORD works righteousness
and justice for all the oppressed.
He made known his ways to Moses,
his deeds to the people of Israel:
The LORD is compassionate and gracious,
slow to anger, abounding in love.
He will not always accuse,
nor will he harbour his anger forever;
he does not treat us as our sins deserve
or repay us according to our iniquities.
For as high as the heavens are above the earth,
so great is his love for those who fear him;
as far as the east is from the west,

so far has he removed our transgressions from us.
As a father has compassion on his children,
so the LORD has compassion on those who fear him;
for he knows how we are formed,
he remembers that we are dust.
As for man, his days are like grass,
he flourishes like a flower of the field;
the wind blows over it and it is gone,
and its place remembers it no more.
But from everlasting to everlasting
the LORD's love is with those who fear him,
and his righteousness with their children's children-
with those who keep his covenant
and remember to obey his precepts.
The LORD has established his throne in heaven,
and his kingdom rules over all.
Praise the LORD, you his angels,
you mighty ones who do his bidding,
who obey his word.
Praise the LORD, all his heavenly hosts,
you his servants who do his will.
Praise the LORD, all his works
everywhere in his dominion.
Praise the LORD, O my soul.

Psalm 103

LOOKING AT THE PSALMS

The book of the psalms is a collection of songs, expressions to God of prayer and praise. They often convey professions of faith and trust, and are mostly written by David, whose life is recorded in 1 and 2 Samuel. Because the psalmists expressed their feelings and emotions in their writings we can easily relate to them. They teach us about our inner selves and inspire us in our personal relationships with God. They point backwards to historical events, forward to the coming of Jesus and to God himself.

1. What would you say to someone who says 'I struggle to feel like praising God on a Sunday morning – I often feel tired, stressed out by what has happened in the week and preoccupied with planning Sunday lunch.'

HOW DOES THIS **2.** In verses 1–2 David starts off by talking to himself, encouraging himself to praise God. Dr Martin Lloyd Jones has said:
APPLY TO ME

'Have you realised that most of your unhappiness in life is due to the fact that you are listening to yourself instead of talking to yourself? You have to take yourself in hand. You have to address yourself, preach to yourself, question yourself. The essence of the matter is to understand that this self of ours, this other man within us; has got to be handled.'

How do you feel about this quotation? When was the last time you needed to give yourself a good talking to?

HOW DOES THIS **3.** If you had not become a Christian how do you think your life would have been different? What are you most grateful to God for?
APPLY TO ME

4. In verses 1–5 David counts his blessings, making a list of all he has as a result of his relationship with God. Rewrite his list in your own words.

WHAT DOES **5.** In verses 6–8 David moves from personal praise to directing others to praise God. He does this by remembering how
SEARCH
THE BIBLE SAY? God revealed himself to Moses. This is a direct quotation from Exodus 34 which we looked at in study 2. Close your Bibles and see how many of the seven characteristics of God you can you remember, then compare these with the ones mentioned in Psalm 103.

6. The centre of the psalm in verses 8–12 focuses on God's love towards us. He had mercy on us and does not treat us as our sins deserve. How did God ultimately forgive our sins and remove them from us?

7. Which of the group members can remember the names of their great-grandparents? What will our great-grandchildren, or great-nephews and nieces, remember about us? How does this make you feel?

8. Read verses 13–18 again. How can these verses comfort and encourage us?

9. The psalm began with David commanding his own soul to worship God. In verses 19-22, the awesome scope of the praise God deserves is highlighted. How should this picture of the universe praising God redefine our view of praise at a service?

HOW DOES THIS
APPLY TO ME **10.** David begins and ends the psalm motivating himself to praise God. However, this public psalm was also recorded to motivate others. Think of practical ways to stir up spiritual passion in your life when you are feeling apathetic. How can we follow David's lead and help one another to stay passionate for God?

WORSHIP

Go around the group sharing your favourite lyrics from a worship song or hymn and the reason why they help you to praise God.

Why do we often use the word 'worship' synonymously with singing? Discuss other ways to worship God.

Write a psalm as a group in 'consequences' style. Each member writes two lines expressing their response to God, folds the paper so that it can't be seen, and passes it around. When all members have written their lines, somebody should read it to the group.

DURING THE WEEK

Every morning, read Psalm 103 as a reminder to yourself to praise God.

Every night before going to sleep, write a journal recording all the things you can thank God for from that day.

FOR FURTHER STUDY

Job 40:1 – 42:6. This parallels our passage by focussing on God's greatness, as opposed to Job's own insignificance, and God's love and faithfulness.

Book to read:

John Piper	*When I don't desire God*	Crossway
Peter Lewis	*The Glory of Christ*	Paternoster
Ravi Zacharias	*Recapture the wonder*	Integrity

THE HUMAN GOD

AIM

Aim: To marvel at and gain comfort from the huge leap that God took in becoming human

TO SET THE SCENE

As people arrive, give them secret slips of paper with a character on it. Once the game starts, the members have to impersonate these individuals or types of people until everybody has been identified. Reflect what it would be like to spend a day or a year living the life of these characters.

READ THE PASSAGE TOGETHER

In the beginning was the Word, and the Word was with God, and the Word was God. He was with God in the beginning.

Through him all things were made; without him nothing was made that has been made. In him was life, and that life was the light of men. The light shines in the darkness, but the darkness has not understood it.

There came a man who was sent from God; his name was John. He came as a witness to testify concerning that light, so that through him all men might believe. He himself was not the light; he came only as a witness to the light. The true light that gives light to every man was coming into the world.

He was in the world, and though the world was made through him, the world did not recognize him. He came to that which was his own, but his own did not receive him. Yet to all who received him, to those who believed in his name, he gave the right to become children of God—children born not of natural descent, nor of human decision or a husband's will, but born of God.

The Word became flesh and made his dwelling among us. We have seen his glory, the glory of the One and Only,who came from the Father, full of grace and truth.

John testifies concerning him. He cries out, saying, "This was he of whom I said, 'He who comes after me has surpassed me because he was before me.'" From the fullness of his grace we have all received one blessing after another. For the law was given through Moses; grace and truth came through Jesus Christ. No-one has ever seen God, but God the One and Only, who is at the Father's side, has made him known.

John 1:1–18

LOOKING AT THE GOSPEL OF JOHN

John was an eyewitness of Jesus' life and was referred to as 'the disciple whom Jesus loved.' He writes his gospel to Greek-speaking Jews around the world to convince them that Jesus is the Son of God and that true life can only be found through relationship with him.

John's Gospel is unique as he does not draw on the same sources as the synoptic gospels (Matthew, Mark, and Luke). John borrowed the everyday language of the Greeks and courageously and radically used it to explain to his readers the significance of Jesus' coming to earth.

1. 'Bill is thinking about moving house. He wants to think strategically about where he lives, to maximise his usefulness for God's work. He could move to a predominantly Asian area but is worried that he wouldn't fit in. He could move downtown but is worried about street crime. He could move to an upper-class area but is worried about becoming a snob.' What lessons can Bill learn from Jesus' coming to earth from heaven?

WHAT DOES **2.** What sacrifices do you think Jesus made by becoming human? What do you think motivated him? You might find help in **THE BIBLE SAY?** Philippians 2:1–11.

WHAT DOES **THE BIBLE SAY?** **3.** Remember back to the first study on Genesis 1:1–3. What similarities do you notice between that passage and John 1:1–5?

WHAT DOES **SEARCH** **THE BIBLE SAY?** **4.** Read John 1:1–5 and John 1:14. Substitute 'Jesus' where it says 'the Word' in verses 1–5 and then write down all the different things these verses claim about Jesus. Which of these is hardest to understand?

WHAT DOES **SEARCH** **THE BIBLE SAY?** **5.** Read John 1:6–9. What was John the Baptist's role? How would you respond to someone saying: 'Christians are narrow-minded bigots for believing that everybody should believe in Jesus and that he is the true light for all people.'

6. What do verses 10–13 teach us about how to become a child of God?

7. How could these verses help someone who says: 'I must be a Christian as I was brought up in a Christian home?'

WHO IS JESUS?
People today still struggle to accept that Jesus was truly God in human form. This passage is one of many that clearly state who Jesus is. Other passages include Hebrews 1:1–4, Colossians 1:15–20 and John 5:19–27. Although Jesus never said 'I am God', he clearly claims direct access to the Father, the ability to forgive sins and to be worthy of worship. The Jewish leaders understood his claim to be God and executed him on a blasphemy charge.

C.S. Lewis famously offered three possibilities. Jesus could have been a lunatic, who thought he was God but was deluded. Alternatively Jesus was a liar, deliberately pretending to be God to deceive people. The only other possibility was that Jesus was truly Lord and was telling the truth.

When explaining who Jesus is to non-Christians, this Lord/liar/lunatic option often helps. You can also point them to the passages above.

HOW DOES THIS / APPLY TO ME **8.** Having understood that God became human, like us, and that Jesus is God, the following story helps us to realise that Jesus is uniquely able to sympathise with us in every situation. How does this make you feel?

Get hold of a copy of John Stott's *The Cross of Christ* (IVP) and read the story on page 336.

9. Compare this picture of the human God with that of the faithful God we looked at in the last study. How can both pictures help us in our prayer life?

HOW DOES THIS / APPLY TO ME **10.** Which of the following struggles do you face and how can Jesus sympathise with and help you?

- ▶ Being misunderstood by people around you?
- ▶ Feeling overwhelmed in busyness?
- ▶ Having your efforts at work go by unnoticed?
- ▶ Feeling 'It's not fair'?
- ▶ Being tempted to do wrong?

WORSHIP

Read, sing or listen to the song *The Servant King* and allow it to inspire your group prayer time.

Begin your prayer time by reading aloud Hebrews 4:14–16 together.

DURING THE WEEK

Read through the Gospel of John, noting all the human difficulties Jesus faces in his lifetime. If you read it through in one sitting, it should take less than an hour.

Pray for any friends who are going through difficult circumstances.

Jesus was prepared to cross cultural barriers in order to bring us salvation. During the week, visit a neighbour who is from a different generation or ethnic background to yourself. Think about how you could show them friendship.

FOR FURTHER STUDY

Jesus was both man and God. To what degree was he fully God and fully man? Study this debate with help from a systematic theology such as Wayne Grudem's *Biblical Theology* (IVP) or *Introduction to Christian Theology* by Alister McGrath (Blackwells).

Books to read:

Philip Yancey	*The Jesus I never knew*	Zondervan
Lee Strobel	*The case for Christ*	Zondervan
Tim Chester	*Delighting in the Trinity*	Monarch
N.T. Wright	*Who is Jesus?*	SPCK

THE SOVEREIGN GOD

Aim: To acknowledge that God is control over the universe and can be trusted whatever the circumstances

TO SET THE SCENE

Imagine that two of the main leaders of your church are imprisoned and awaiting sentence for saying that Jesus is the only way to God. You have been asked to pray as a group. How do you feel? What would you pray for? What Bible passages would you read? What practical steps would you take?

READ THE PASSAGE TOGETHER

On their release, Peter and John went back to their own people and reported all that the chief priests and elders had said to them. When they heard this, they raised their voices together in prayer to God. "Sovereign Lord," they said, "you made the heaven and the earth and the sea, and everything in them. You spoke by the Holy Spirit through the mouth of your servant, our father David:

" 'Why do the nations rage and the peoples plot in vain? The kings of the earth take their stand and the rulers gather together against the Lord and against his Anointed One.'

Indeed Herod and Pontius Pilate met together with the Gentiles and the people of Israel in this city to conspire against your holy servant Jesus, whom you anointed. They did what your power and will had decided beforehand should happen. Now, Lord, consider their threats and enable your servants to speak your word with great boldness. Stretch out your hand to heal and perform miraculous signs and wonders through the name of your holy servant Jesus."

After they prayed, the place where they were meeting was shaken. And they were all filled with the Holy Spirit and spoke the word of God boldly.

Acts 4:23–31

INTRODUCTION TO ACTS

Acts describes how Jesus continued his ministry on earth through his church and the Holy Spirit after he has ascended to heaven. It is the follow-up to Luke's gospel, written by a doctor who meticulously investigated the life of Jesus through eye-witness testimonies (Lk. 1:1–4).

The book describes the explosion of Christianity throughout the world 'beginning in Jerusalem' and ending up at 'the ends of the earth' (Acts1:8).

There is a strong emphasis on the Holy Spirit equipping the church to proclaim the message of Jesus, even in the face of severe persecution and suffering. This book helps us to communicate the Christian faith in a number of different settings. We need to learn from the early church how to be faithful to the gospel and yet adapt how we present it in a variety of contexts.

1. The disciples have just healed a crippled man in the name of Jesus. Acts reports that, because of this miracle and Peter's address to the crowds, the number of Christians grew to five thousand, and Peter and John were imprisoned. Can you think of times in your own life when boldness for the gospel and blessing in ministry have gone hand in hand with persecution?

2. 'Eva became a Christian in miraculous circumstances and saw many of her friends also come to faith at her baptism a few weeks later. However, when she was suddenly made redundant at work, she stopped coming to church, saying that she could no longer believe in a God who would allow this to happen.' To what extent can you sympathise with Eva's predicament?

HOW DOES THIS **3.** What would be a typical summary of your prayers? How long do you spend focussing on who God is, what he has APPLY TO ME done in the past, Scripture and personal requests? How does this compare with the believers' prayer in this chapter?

WHAT DOES
SEARCH
THE BIBLE SAY?

4. The believers begin their prayer by recognising who God is.

What aspects of God's character do they praise and why? Which of our earlier passages does this remind you of?

5. How should beginning our prayers with the words 'Sovereign Lord' affect what we then ask God for?

6. We have seen in previous studies how remembering God's faithfulness in the past inspires our faith. How is this true for the early Christians?

WHAT DOES
SEARCH
THE BIBLE SAY?

7. The early Christians quoted Scripture in their prayer. Looking back to David's psalm, they understood that he was prophesying the execution of Jesus. How did this help them face persecution and how can it help us today?

WHO IS IN CONTROL?

The time-old question of God's sovereignty and human freedom has perplexed thinkers throughout history. This passage argues that Herod and Pilate did what God's 'power and will had decided beforehand should happen.' If that is true can they, Judas Iscariot or for that matter any of us be held responsible for what we do?

This incredibly complex question cannot be answered in a few sentences. But it is worth noting that the Bible teaches both that God is sovereignly in control and that humans are responsible for their actions. As far as Herod and Pilate were concerned, they were not robots, simply following instructions – they decided their own actions. But from God's perspective, they were using their freedom in such a way that it accomplished God's purposes. The Bible does not resolve this apparent contradiction but rather asks us to hold in tension both God's kingship and human freedom and responsibility.

8. What is the disciples' main request in this passage and why is it surprising? How does it compare to what we would ask for in the same situation?

WHAT DOES
SEARCH
THE BIBLE SAY?

9. In this country, we are not under threat of torture or imprisonment for telling others about Jesus. Why do you think the church is nevertheless often timid in its evangelism?

APPLY THIS TO
MY CHURCH

10. How do God's sovereign control of the world and our mandate to tell the world about our faith go hand in hand? Look at Matthew 28:18–20.

WORSHIP

Divide the group into two and take turns to read 1 Peter 4:12–19 to each other for encouragement.

We too can use Scripture to launch our prayers. To start you off, take the following verses as launches for your prayer time today.

Genesis 1:27–28
Exodus 33:19–20
Deuteronomy 6:13–14
Psalm 103:11–12
John 1:16

DURING THE WEEK

Look on the internet for information about Christians who are in prison for their faith. Write down their names somewhere prominent and remember to pray for them.

www.releaseinternational.org
www.persecution.org
www.opendoors.org

Think of five friends who are not yet Christians and determine to take a step to introduce them to Jesus. Perhaps this means praying for them, inviting them for coffee or dinner, taking them along to a church service or Alpha course or giving them a book about your faith.

FOR FURTHER STUDY

Look through the book of Acts, noting references to the Holy Spirit. What proportion of these also mentions evangelism as a result of being filled with the Holy Spirit?

Books to read:

Rebecca Manley-Pippert	*Out of the saltshaker*	IVP
P. Yancey	*Reaching for the invisible God*	Hodder & Stoughton
C.S. Lewis	*The problem of pain*	Collins
J.I. Packer	*Evangelism and the sovereignty of God*	IVP

THE MISSIONARY GOD

Aim: To understand how at the end of history God will reign supreme and that now is our opportunity to prepare the world to meet him

TO SET THE SCENE

Give each person a large sheet of sketching paper and some coloured pens. Ask them to draw their picture of Paradise. Ask each member to explain their pictures to the group.

READ THE PASSAGE TOGETHER

Then I saw a new heaven and a new earth, for the first heaven and the first earth had passed away, and there was no longer any sea. I saw the Holy City, the new Jerusalem, coming down out of heaven from God, prepared as a bride beautifully dressed for her husband. And I heard a loud voice from the throne saying, "Now the dwelling of God is with men, and he will live with them. They will be his people, and God himself will be with them and be their God. He will wipe every tear from their eyes. There will be no more death or mourning or crying or pain, for the old order of things has passed away."

He who was seated on the throne said, "I am making everything new!" Then he said, "Write this down, for these words are trustworthy and true."

He said to me: "It is done. I am the Alpha and the Omega, the Beginning and the End. To him who is thirsty I will give to drink without cost from the spring of the water of life. He who overcomes will inherit all this, and I will be his God and he will be my son. But the cowardly, the unbelieving, the vile, the murderers, the sexually immoral, those who practice magic arts, the idolaters and all liars—their place will be in the fiery lake of burning sulphur. This is the second death."

One of the seven angels who had the seven bowls full of the seven last plagues came and said to me, "Come, I will show you the bride, the wife of the Lamb." And he carried me away in the Spirit to a mountain great and high, and showed me the Holy City, Jerusalem, coming down out of heaven from God. It shone with the glory of God, and its brilliance was like that of a very precious jewel, like a jasper, clear as crystal. It had a great, high wall with twelve gates, and with twelve angels at the gates. On the gates were written the names of the twelve tribes of Israel. There were three gates on the east, three on the north, three on the south and three on the west. The wall of the city had twelve foundations, and on them were the names of the twelve apostles of the Lamb.

The angel who talked with me had a measuring rod of gold to measure the city, its gates and its walls. The city was laid out like a square, as long as it was wide. He measured the city with the rod and found it to be 12,000 stadia in length, and as wide and high as it is long. He measured its wall and it was 144 cubits thick, by man's measurement, which the angel was using. The wall was made of jasper, and the city of pure gold, as pure as glass. The foundations of the city walls were decorated with every kind of precious stone. The first foundation was jasper, the second sapphire, the third chalcedony, the fourth emerald, the fifth sardonyx, the sixth carnelian, the seventh chrysolite, the eighth beryl, the ninth topaz, the tenth chrysoprase, the eleventh jacinth, and the twelfth amethyst. The twelve gates were twelve pearls, each gate made of a single pearl. The great street of the city was of pure gold, like transparent glass.

I did not see a temple in the city, because the Lord God Almighty and the Lamb are its temple. The city does not need the sun or the moon to shine on it, for the glory of God gives it light, and the Lamb is its lamp. The nations will walk by its light, and the kings of the earth will bring their splendour into it. On no day will its gates ever be shut, for there will be no night there. The glory and honour of the nations will be brought into it. Nothing impure will ever enter it, nor will anyone who does what is shameful or deceitful, but only those whose names are written in the Lamb's book of life.

Revelation 21

LOOKING AT REVELATION

Revelation is often treated like a book written in a secret code, but it was written to bless, not bemuse, Christians. In his introduction, the apostle John tells us that he has been given a revelation of Jesus to help the church face what is about to happen. In the context of the early church, this was to be extreme persecution and God gave the church a majestic picture of himself to sustain them through times of trouble. The book contains letters, prophecy and a style of literature known as apocalyptic, which sought to reveal what God was doing in history, particularly how he would judge evil and reward the righteous. You can see this style at work in the second half of the book of Daniel. Although this style is difficult for us to understand, an important principle in understanding the Bible is to let straightforward passages interpret the less clear ones. So it seems sensible to look to the gospels and the epistles to give us guidelines for understanding the end of history, rather than relying on the figurative and pictorial language of Revelation. What Revelation does provide are powerful pictures to help us experience God's glory and his kingly rule over history.

1. Divide into two teams. One team has to think of films, books or television shows that describe a positive future for the human race. The other team has to think of examples of negative pictures of the future. Which picture of the future do you think is more prevalent and why?

APPLY THIS TO **2.** Our studies have taken us on a journey from a garden at the beginning of time (Genesis 1 in Session 1) to the end of time. MY CHURCH Indeed God is described as the Alpha and the Omega in verse 6. However, our destiny is not back in a garden but in a city – the New Jerusalem. What are the implications of this and how does it make you feel?

3. God made two people to live in the Garden of Eden. However, by the end of time, it is clear that he is catering for millions of people who will come from every nation (v26). Remembering the last study (Session 6) how has this been achieved?

4. We have also considered God as a human and suffering God (Session 5), who sympathises with us in our difficulties and who asks us to face persecution for his sake (Session 6). What comfort can we find in verses 1–7?

5. According to verse 8, what will happen to those who do not believe in God? Why is this such an unpopular doctrine in the church today? What should knowing this motivate us to do?

6. In session 2 we saw how Moses pleaded with God for his presence to go with them. When God showed his glory to Moses his face shone. How does this passage emphasise the presence of God with his people and his glory?

7. What does the 'glory and honour of the nations' (v26) mean? How does this affect the way we think about specific nations: think of Islamic majority countries like Iraq, relatively insignificant places like Albania, or the world superpower, America?

8. Summarise what we have learned over the past six sessions to show what it means that God is a missionary God.

9. What would you say to the following people?

'I am not looking forward to heaven – I like my life as it is.'

'I am looking forward to heaven – peace and quiet at last.'

10. Which aspects of God's character have become more real to you in these sessions? How has this changed the way you worship, pray and relate to God and others?

WORSHIP

Take a look at the labels on your clothes and accessories, or at the objects, books and pictures around the room, to find out where they have been produced. Pray for those countries.

Switch on BBC News 24 or look up world headlines on Teletext. Pray about global events.

Write a card or letter of encouragement to one of your church's mission partners.

DURING THE WEEK

Sign on to a missionary agency's email list to receive regular prayer updates from around the world.

Buy a world map to put up in your kitchen to help you follow world events and commit to watching the news, or buy a newspaper regularly through the week.

FOR FURTHER STUDY

Make a list of other aspects of God's nature and character that we have not explored. Make a plan to study them over the next few weeks.

Books to read:

Robin Wells and George Verwer	*My rights, my God*	Monarch
Elizabeth Elliot	*Shadow of the Almighty*	Authentic
John Piper	*Let the nations be glad*	IVP
Samuel Escobar	*Time for mission*	IVP

LEADERS' GUIDE

TO HELP YOU LEAD

You may have led a group many times before or this may be your first time. Here is some advice on how to lead these studies:

▶ As a group leader, you don't have to be an expert or a lecturer. You are there to facilitate the learning of the group members – helping them to discover for themselves the wisdom in God's word. You should not be doing most of the talking or dishing out the answers, whatever the group expects of you!

▶ You do need to be aware of the group's dynamics, however. People can be quite quick to label themselves and each other in a group situation. One person might be seen as the expert, another the moaner who always has something to complain about. One person may be labelled as quiet and not be expected to contribute; another person may always jump in with something to say. Be aware of the different types of individuals in the group, but don't allow the labels to stick. You may need to encourage those who find it hard to get a word in, and quieten down those who always have something to say. Talk to members between sessions to find out how they feel about the group.

▶ The sessions are planned to try to engage every member in actively learning. Of course you cannot force anyone to take part if they don't want to, but it won't be too easy to be a spectator. Activities that ask everyone to write down something, or to talk in twos and then report back to the group, are there for a reason. They give everyone space to think and form their opinion, even if not everyone voices it out loud.

▶ Do adapt the sessions for your group as you feel is appropriate. Some groups may know each other very well and will be prepared to talk at a deep level. New groups may take a bit of time to get to know each other before making themselves vulnerable, but encourage members to share their lives with each other.

▶ Encourage a number of replies to each question. The study is not about finding a single right answer, but about sharing experiences and thoughts in order to find out how to apply the Bible to people's lives. When brainstorming, don't be too quick to evaluate the contributions. Write everything down and then have a look to see which suggestions are worth keeping.

▶ Similarly encourage everyone to ask questions, to voice doubts and to discuss difficulties. Some parts of the Bible are hard to understand. Sometimes the Christian faith throws up paradoxes. Painful things happen to us that make it difficult to see what God is doing. A housegroup should be a safe place to express all this. If discussion doesn't resolve the issue, send everyone away to pray about it, and ask your minister for advice!

▶ Give yourself time in the week to read through the Bible passage and the questions. Read the Leaders' notes for the session, as different ways of presenting the questions are sometimes suggested. However, during the session, don't be too quick to come in with the answer – sometimes we need space to think.

▶ Delegate as much as you like! The easiest activities to delegate are reading the text and the worship suggestions, but there are other ways to involve the group members. Giving people responsibility can help them own the session much more.

▶ Pray for group members by name, that God would meet with them during the week. Pray for the group session that it will be a constructive and helpful time. Ask the Lord to equip you as you lead the group.

THE STRUCTURE OF EACH SESSION
Feedback: find out what people remember from the previous session and if they have been able to act during the week on what was discussed last time.

To set the scene: an activity or a question to get everyone thinking about the subject to be studied.

Bible reading: it's important actually to read the passage you are studying during the session. Ask someone to prepare this in advance or go around the group reading a verse or two each. But don't assume everyone will be happy to read out loud.

Questions and activities: these are designed to promote discussion on how to apply what the passage says to your individual/group situation.

During the week: a specific task to do during the week to help people put into practice what they have learned.

Prayer: suggestions for creative prayer. Use these suggestions alongside other group expressions of worship such as singing. Add a prayer time with opportunities to pray for group members and their families and friends.

GROUND RULES
How do people know what is expected of them during your meetings? Is it ever discussed, or do they just pick up clues from each other? You may find it helpful to discuss some ground rules for the housegroup at the start of this course, even if your group has been going a long time. This also gives you an opportunity to talk about how you, as the leader, see the group. Ask everyone to think about what they want to get out of the course. How do they want the group to work? What values do they want to be part of the group's experience: honesty, respect, confidentiality?

How do they want their contributions to be treated? You could ask everyone to write down three ground rules on slips of paper and put them in a bowl. Pass the bowl around the group. Each person takes out a rule and reads it, and someone collates the list. Discuss the ground rules that have been suggested and come up with a top five. This method enables everyone to contribute fairly anonymously. Alternatively, if your group are all quite vocal, have a straight discussion about it!

ICONS

 The aim of the session

 Engaging with the world

 Investigate what else the Bible says

 How does this apply to me?

 What about my church?

NB not all questions in each session are covered, some are self-explanatory

SESSION 1

YOU WILL NEED:
A selection of 'creating' materials, such as LEGO bricks, newspapers or tins.

TO SET THE SCENE:
However hard we work at our 'creations', we cannot come close to the amazing creation of God. We may complain about our lack of resources but God created everything out of nothing. His power just by speaking is incredible. The detail and the variety of all we see around us is awe-inspiring. As the teams compare their finished products, note how people feel about what they have created. How much more must God care about his creation!

1. Our picture of God is often too small. We often struggle to believe that God can answer our prayers, or that God makes a difference in the challenges we face. However, remembering that he is also the God who created the world with just a breath challenges us to increase our view of him.

2. God creates different things on different days. But there is also a structure within the week. God separates things in the first three days and he fills them on the next three days. On the seventh day, God rests.

FORMLESS AND EMPTY	
Separation	**Filling**
Day 1 Light and darkness	Day 4 Sun and stars
Day 2 Sky and sea	Day 5 Birds and fish
Day 3 Sea and land	Day 6 Animals and man
Day 7 Sabbath	

3. Human beings are created last, as the pinnacle of God's work. Uniquely God says 'let us' (1:26) before creating human beings. Only human beings are described as being made in the image of God. At the end of each day of creation, we are told 'God saw all that he had made and it was good.' After creating human beings, we are told that it was 'very good' (1:31). God gave human beings unique authority and responsibility over the earth. God rests after making human beings now that his work of creation is complete.

4. Looking at the options presented:

a) The Bible is very clear that God is Spirit and he is everywhere: in other words, he does not have a body.

b) This is a possible reading of the text but, even after the fall, we are still in the image of God, even in our sinfulness.

c) The Bible teaches clearly that there is only one God.

d) This seems to be the most likely explanation, as immediately after the statement that God was to make us in his image, he commands the humans to rule over creation. This fits a custom that we know about the ancient Near East. A king would construct a statue of himself in a city that he had conquered to remind the inhabitant of his power and rule over them. In the same way, man is called the image of God because he was supposed to represent the rule of God over creation

5. All people everywhere are made in God's image, independent of ethnic or economic background, abilities or orientation. Looking at ourselves should give us an incredible sense of value and self worth. As we look at others, we should appreciate and respect them as being made by God.

6. Our rule over the earth is to be an image of God's rule over the universe. There should be no exploitation of people or resources, but we need to develop a sense of social and environmental responsibility and compassion. This should affect our lifestyle; from recycling to job choices, from politics to carbon emissions.

7. Genesis 1 teaches us two important factors. It helps us understand that we are loved and valued, giving us a sense of self worth and belonging. It also helps us understand that we have a task and a responsibility, giving us a sense of purpose. Tactfully and compassionately we can talk about God's great love for everyone and try to show this man that there is another dimension to his life that can be fulfilled.

8. The point of this discussion is not to prove your own case but to understand that both arguments have their strengths and weaknesses. Explore these in a friendly debate.

9. There are many illustrations that may help your neighbour see the step of faith he is taking by believing in 'chance': William Paley's famous example is that if you found a watch you would not assume that it was a product of chance and time but would assume a designer. The incredible complexities of the human body seem to point to a design rather than chance. Equally the feeling of joy when we hold a newborn baby, the awe we feel looking out at a starry night, are clues that there is more to life than can be measured in a test tube. Even non-Christian scientists admit to falling in love or teaching their children right from wrong.

10. Many of our insecurities can be challenged as we realise that we are created by the One who made the stars, the mountains and the birds. Without the need to worry about 're-creating' ourselves to fit in with media images, we are free to care about God and others.

YOU WILL NEED

The trailer of the film *Castaway* or *Lost in Translation*. (www.HollywoodJesus.com)

TO SET THE SCENE

In both these films, the main character is desperately lonely as all the supports for a normal life have been removed. We experience loneliness at many levels: feeling left out at school, losing a job, finding our feet in a new job or community, watching our children leave home, facing bereavement or divorce. In all these situations, we crave companionship and hope for the future. It is exactly these things that Moses will show as he turns to God in his loneliness. However, we do not always turn to God in our loneliness. Sometimes he feels far away, and we try to rely on our own strength. Encourage the group members to be open and honest in their struggles and to pray for each other.

1. Moses faced dissent everywhere. His brother Aaron instigated the setting up of the golden calf (Ex. 32). Aaron and Moses' sister Miriam turned against him (Num. 12). The people of Israel continually complained against God and Moses.

2. Moses asked God for reassurance of his presence, not only for his benefit but also that God would be honoured amongst the nations. God answered Moses' request by showing him part of his glory.

3. We often talk about the glory of a victorious sports team. The word 'glory' is also banded around at the last night of the Proms. God's glory does not come from his accomplishments but from his character, and so when Moses sees God's glory, he actually experiences God passing by, proclaiming his name (34:6). The holiness of God is so dangerous that no-one can see God and live, so God shields Moses in the cleft of the rock, covering him with his hand.

4. God is both our Lord and Master and yet our Saviour and Friend. When we pray, we must remember both of these aspects. We can call him Father, but only in the name of Jesus, through his saving work on the cross.

6. Moses realises his own sinfulness in the light of God's glory. He bows to the ground in worship and asks for forgiveness for himself and the nation. He also asks for God to own his people, both now and in the future.

7. Just as a parent with young children asks for obedience in order to protect the children from harm, so God as a loving Father and King demonstrates care for his people by asking obedience from them. Just as a husband promises exclusive love for his wife because of his love for her, so God proves the extent of his love through his jealousy for our worship.

10. Here are a few hints:

'I am too bad to become a Christian. I could never measure up to God's standards.'

It is exactly because we are so bad that God's holiness demanded the perfect sacrifice of his Son in our place. God's love for us is not dependent on our performance: rather it is a free gift of grace.

'I don't need to become a Christian. I live a good life and help others where ever I can.'

This person can be commended for trying to help others. But why do they do that? Do they believe they will get to heaven that way? What evidence is that based upon? If they are interested in your views, you can explain that compared to God's perfection, none of us are good enough. If they are really trying to be as good as possible, why not offer to help them by studying Jesus' life with them, as someone of whom it is said that he did no wrong?

SESSION 3

YOU WILL NEED

Pen and paper.

TO SET THE SCENE

Moses is preparing his people for the future. This exercise helps us to put ourselves in his shoes and consider the challenges facing the church of tomorrow.

1. Issues such as a multi-faith society, childhood obesity, internet pornography, social acceptance of homosexual practice, debt and consumerism are possible discussion starters. The next generation will face more acute environmental challenges, the possible prohibition of evangelism, further genetic advances and the ethical issues this provokes, amongst others.

2. Some would use this passage to justify a prosperity approach to the gospel, that all Christians will be wealthy and healthy if they follow him. However, God is equally present with the Israelites in the wilderness and blesses them there, and he is at pains to warn them that there are other risks to their faith in comfortable surroundings.

3. The first is (vv10–12) the danger of affluence for a refugee nation suddenly inheriting a land flowing with milk and honey. This brings with it the risk of forgetting that God is their Provider. The second danger (vv13–19) is the temptation to follow the gods of their new neighbours.

4. Moses emphasises that there is only one true God (v4), that God is worthy of total devotion (v5) and that the people should weave God's truth into their lives through daily remembrance of Scripture.

5. In a context of a culture that had many gods, the Israelites were set apart by believing in only one God. He was to be their sole object of worship.

6. Our culture emphasises love as a feeling or as a physical act. Even the fact that we are commanded to love God emphasises that this type of love is to be an act of the will, a decision and a commitment. It is not just our emotions that are involved but our whole being; our intellect, dreams, plans and daily lifestyles etc.

7. a) This is partly right. God expects and deserves our total devotion. We should have no love left for any other deity – sin, money, football, status… . However, far from leaving us devoid of affection for people around us, we are commanded to love them as part of our love for God.

b) Affirm that we go through emotional seasons in our relationship with God, and that maturing is a good thing. However, it should not mean that we allow our love for God to be diluted. In fact, this is disobedience to this command.

8. Moses is very clear that we are to obey the commandments ourselves and also that we are responsible for passing on the faith to the next generation. You may find it helpful to read together the list in the box as a summary.

10. This view is rife in our multicultural society. It implies that there is only a surface-level distinction between the religions. It is an attempt to minimise the tensions between the religions, but patronises people from all religious backgrounds. Christians need to show respect for people of all faith, to be able to discuss the fundamental differences between the religions and still assert that there is only one true God, and the only way to him is through Jesus.

SESSION 4

YOU WILL NEED

A tray of twenty different small items, such as keys, screws, paperclips etc, and a towel to cover; pen and paper for each group member.

TO SET THE SCENE

Memory was a key theme in the previous study, where Moses encourages the people to remember God whatever their circumstances and to pass on the faith to the next generation. The theme is also important in this psalm as our worship for God will grow cold unless we continually remember his faithfulness. God chooses not to remember our sins but has mercy on us, promising to remember us from everlasting to everlasting and for future generations. In this game, most individuals will not be able to remember all twenty items. However, as a group, you probably can. This applies to our spiritual lives: we need each other to help us remember all God's blessings.

1. We can all relate to this to some degree. Many of us struggle to do anything unless we feel like it and so, if we don't feel like praising God, then we don't. Others of us simply go through the motions and sing the words in services without them really engaging our minds or emotions. We need to look to the Bible to help us overcome these barriers, and we can find a lot of help from the Psalmists, who are very honest about their feelings and still relate to God in worship.

2. David is motivating himself to praise God, and praise God more whole-heartedly. We will learn through this psalm some strategies for deepening our own worship.

3. If group members struggle to think of any differences that being a Christian has made to their lives, this should disturb us. Give the group members some quiet time to reflect and encourage them to be imaginative about the directions they could have taken without God.

6. God not only forgives our sins but separates them from us. This is wonderfully illustrated in the Day of Atonement with the setting free of the scapegoat (Lev.16:20–24). In parallel, Jesus himself was taken outside of the city to be executed and took on himself the sin of the world.

8. David knows that our lives are short in comparison to the eternal nature of God. He describes us as grass and dust. However, he triumphantly celebrates God's everlasting love to us, despite our otherwise insignificant lives. David also recognises that God's faithfulness is not limited to his generation. We are a fulfilment of this promise.

9. The universe was designed to bring glory to God and our lives of praise are to be an integral part of this. When we attend large worship conferences, we rejoice in feeling part of a greater body praising God. However, this is permanently true as we join with all nature whenever and wherever we glorify God.

YOU WILL NEED

Small pieces of paper with names on it. A CD of the song *The Servant King* (Graham Kendrick) or a copy of the words. A copy of John Stott's *The Cross of Christ* (IVP).

TO SET THE SCENE

For this game use famous celebrities such as the Queen, David Beckham, Richard Branson, Bill Gates, Madonna, Julia Roberts and Tom Cruise. Also use poor people such as a traveller, a third world orphan, a homeless man, Mother Teresa. The point of this game is to experience putting yourself in someone else's shoes and discover the cultural and social challenges this involves.

1. Many Christians have taken inspiration from Jesus' humility in leaving the glory of heaven to be born in the 'squalor of a borrowed stable.' For example, missionaries choose to leave the comforts of Western living to live in shanty towns in India or work amongst street children in Bolivia. Whenever we make a cross cultural move, we must learn how to emulate Jesus.

2. Jesus left the splendour and power of heaven to be a vulnerable baby, born into the unfashionable north of a country considered a backwater of the vast Roman Empire. Jesus, the omnipotent God, faced the struggles of human suffering, pain and temptation. He knew the loneliness of misunderstanding from family and the betrayal of close friends. He did this for us and for God's glory.

3. Both start with the words 'In the beginning.' Both recount the story of God's creation. Both emphasise God creating through his word. Both feature the motif of darkness and light. Both recognise that God is the Creator of all things that exist. This is a strange way to start a biography but John wants to show that Jesus is God and that his life on earth needs to be understood in the context of the big picture of the creation of the universe.

4. Probably the most difficult aspect to understand is how Jesus can be with God and be God at the same time. This brings us to the doctrine of the Trinity. There have been hints about the Trinity even in our first study in Genesis 1 where we read that God said 'Let us make man in our image.' Deuteronomy 6:4 emphasised that 'the Lord is One' and the doctrine of the Trinity does not contradict this, as Christians believe that God is one being in three persons.

5. John the Baptist was to prepare the way for Jesus, the coming Messiah. This chapter makes very clear that Jesus' coming was for the whole world. Note the following phrases: 'all men ... true light ... every man.'

In a multicultural society it often seems that the idea of truth is politically incorrect. However, God cannot exist for some people and not others, in the same way that the existence of Paris does not depend on people's cultural beliefs.

6. Jesus acts as a fork in the road: it is our response to him that determines whether we are accepted into God's family or not. These verses show what will happen if we do recognise Jesus as our Lord and God, and if we do not.

7. Verse 12 argues that being born into God's family is not hereditary. This challenged Jewish conceptions of salvation, as many assumed that their ancestry guaranteed their inclusion into God's people. Similarly, we must also understand that at some stage all of us must choose to 'receive and believe' in Jesus for ourselves.

9. God is both the Ruler of the universe to be worshipped and glorified and also the baby in the manger and the Saviour crying in Gethsemane, whom we can turn to in our weakness and distress.

SESSION 6

YOU WILL NEED

Access to the internet to look up information on the persecuted church.

TO SET THE SCENE

This is the situation that is described in Acts 4. It is helpful to realise how scared the Christians would have been and how helpless they would have felt. In the first century, the situation would have been desperate: Israel was still under occupation. The legal system was precarious, prison conditions were poor, the death penalty and other corporal punishments and torture were in regular use and Christians represented a tiny, virtually unknown, minority. The church was only a few weeks old and most of the Christians were very new converts.

1. This is the first miracle that the disciples perform after Jesus' ascension. Filled with the Holy Spirit, Peter is courageous in preaching the gospel to the crowds and to those that bring them to trial. Throughout the book of Acts, we are shown through the lives of Peter, Stephen, Paul and others that great blessing in ministry leads to severe persecution.

2. Many of us find it easy to trust God when all is going well and struggle to trust him when it isn't. It is difficult enough to see the big picture of God's kingship when things are going well, let alone when we are suffering. We need to learn from the myriad of biblical characters who had to trust God in difficult circumstances: characters such as Hannah, Job, Ruth, Abraham, Paul and Jesus.

3. Our prayers are often shopping lists of things we want God to give or do for us. We often pray for our needs rather than praying for God's agenda in the world. The believers in Acts pray with a sense of urgency for God's mission in the world, their prayers are laced with Scripture and they are mindful of the big picture of God's work in history.

4. The believers recognise God's kingship, his work of creation, his inspiration of Scripture, his prophetic voice in the psalms, his guiding hand in the events around the crucifixion and his passion for world mission. There are echoes here of Genesis 1, Deuteronomy 6 and Psalm 103.

5. Recognising God's sovereignty should help us to pray big prayers. We can be inspired to pray with confidence that God is ultimately in charge of the universe and so nothing is too difficult for him. Recognising that God reigns will also inspire us to submit our requests in humility, knowing that the universe exists for God's glory and not for our pleasure.

6. The early Christians look back at the events of the death of Jesus through the lens of Psalm 2. They recognise that God's word was fulfilled, that he keeps his promises and that if God is powerful enough to work through even the schemes of wicked rulers, he is powerful enough for any of the problems they are going to face.

7. The early Christians looked back and saw how God used the suffering of Jesus for his purpose and that he had predicted this hundreds of years beforehand. Equipped with this knowledge, they ask God to look on their own situation of persecution and to give them the courage and power they need to play their part in God's mission.

8. The disciples ask for power for mission. This is surprising as being part of God's mission landed Peter and John in prison. Often when we suffer for doing something for God we have a 'once bitten, twice shy' attitude and change direction. Our prayers focus on personal relief and justice. The persecution the church faced seems to strengthen their resolve, rather than weaken it.

9. It is possible that our timidity is because we are not convinced that the gospel is true and that God is worth proclaiming or that he is in charge of the universe. It may also be due to the subtle influences of our culture, which does not like being told what to do or what to believe, or to an outmoded style of evangelism.

10. The fact that Jesus has authority from God gives us confidence to know that when we do what he says, we will be part of God's work in the world.

SESSION 7

YOU WILL NEED

Coloured pens, sketching paper, access to a television or today's newspapers.

TO SET THE SCENE

It will be interesting to see how many of us still picture paradise as a garden or beach, far away from other people. In this passage we will see a God who is bringing people to live together as the holy bride for his Son, Jesus Christ.

1. *The Matrix, The Day After Tomorrow, Blade Runner, I Robot, 1984* and *The Brave New World* are examples of dark, foreboding images of the future. The *Star Trek* series tends to paint light, clean and positive views of the future.

2. Many of us do not like cities and would rather live in the beauty of the countryside. God uses the picture of a perfect city to describe the future, because ultimately our salvation is communal as well as personal.

3. We saw in the last study the early church's passion for mission, despite persecution and here we see that their labour was not in vain. The Spirit-empowered mission of the church is successful because there are people from every nation gathered together as the people of God.

4. The God who understands our suffering takes the time to wipe away our tears and put an end to all suffering. It is a breathtaking picture of a God who spoke the universe into being, stooping down to wipe the tears away from the eyes of his children.

5. The Bible is clear about eternal judgement, despite our unease at talking about hell. It is true that the language is figurative – nevertheless the metaphor of a fiery lake of burning sulphur is describing pain, torment and suffering as God's judgement on sin is revealed. As we think about this punishment for sin, we must think 'There but for the grace of God go I.' It is only God's mercy that rescued us from the same fate and this should motivate us to share the good news whenever we have the opportunity.

6. We are told that the dwelling of God is now with men (v3), that the whole city shines with the glory of God (v10) and the city is a perfect cube (v16). The only other perfect cube mentioned in the Bible is the Most Holy Place, where God's presence was manifest in the temple. The city needs neither sun nor moon because the glory of God gives it light (v23).

7. There is an emphasis on God's global reign. God deserves praise from all the nations. As we saw in the last session, the disciples were commissioned to go into 'all the nations' (Mt. 28:18–20). Here we see the fruit of that mission. Each nation has intrinsic value to God that will persist even into heaven itself. This should teach us to learn about and value other cultures.

8. We have learned that God created all humanity (Gen. 1) and is present with his people wherever they go, from dry desert to Promised Land (Ex. 34). We have learned that the whole of creation was designed to praise God (Ps. 103). God sent Jesus as a missionary into the world to be the true light of revelation for everyone (Jn. 1), and we too as the church are to take the gospel to all people fearlessly (Acts 4).

9. It is interesting that Jesus' message made the greatest impact on the poor, dispossessed and afflicted. These are the sort of people who would look forward to heaven. Jesus' parable of the great banquet in Luke 14 makes the point that those who have comfortable lives turn down the invitation to heaven while the poor respond to the gracious invitation of the generous host.

The picture of Jerusalem as a bustling city does not sound peaceful or quiet. Although God is the main attraction of heaven, we will also spend eternity with a great multitude of people. This should inspire us to work at our relationships while here on earth.